Throwing the
DIAMOND
HITCH

UNIVERSITY OF CALGARY
Press

Throwing the DIAMOND HITCH

by EMILY URSULIAK

Brave & Brilliant Series
ISSN 2371-7238 (Print) ISSN 2371-7246 (Online)

University of Calgary Press
2500 University Drive NW
Calgary, Alberta
Canada T2N 1N4
press.ucalgary.ca

LIBRARY AND ARCHIVES CANADA CATALOGUING IN PUBLICATION

Ursuliak, Emily, 1988-, author
    Throwing the diamond hitch / by Emily Ursuliak.

(Brave & brilliant series ; no. 2)
Poems.
Issued in print and electronic formats.
ISBN 978-1-55238-922-5 (softcover).—ISBN 978-1-55238-923-2 (PDF).—
ISBN 978-1-55238-924-9 (EPUB).—ISBN 978-1-55238-925-6 (MOBI)

    I. Title. II. Title: Diamond hitch. III. Series: Brave & brilliant
series ; 2

PS8641.R93T57 2017   C811'.6   C2017-900391-7
                                             C2017-900392-5

The University of Calgary Press acknowledges the support of the Government of Alberta through the Alberta Media Fund for our publications. We acknowledge the financial support of the Government of Canada. We acknowledge the financial support of the Canada Council for the Arts for our publishing program.

Printed and bound in Canada by Marquis
♻ This book is printed on Rolland Opaque Smooth paper

Editing by Helen Hajnoczky
Cover design, page design, and typesetting by Melina Cusano

That night we stayed with Margie & Jack in Vancouver and next morning packed gear for the open road —

After lunch at Hope we started over Hope Princeton Highway and stopped after 10 min. to cool —

Reached Summit. Anne in gear looking back.

Our first night out we went several miles past Kuameos and up a side road following a very high narrow canyon with a roaring stream coming down.

That night we camped
on the banks of the Kettle
River beyond Grand Forks —
I have breakfast in a
smoke smudge to keep off
mosquetoes —

We leave the road far below as we
go over the last hump and start
down towards Rossland and Trail —

After following the Kootenay Lake we
climb towards Creston — Below are
irrigated re-claimed farm lands.

We had breakfast
here the first morning
out after we got through
Banff and its Red tape —
Having left at 3.00 A.M.

Cast of Characters

Main Characters

PHYLLIS: Born a prairie girl in Blackfalds, Alberta, she followed her parents to Victoria after they sold their dairy farm and that was where she met Anne. She often goes by "Phyl" for short.

ANNE: Anne lives on the acreage next to Phyl and had come to Canada from London, where she had been training as a nurse.

JASON: A beloved 1927 MG Roadster that Phyllis and Anne saved up for and bought together for $150.

MONTY: The pinto who is Anne's mount for the journey.

PEACHES: The roan horse who Phyllis rides for the trip.

PEDRO: The mischievous packhorse who follows his own whims and hates to have anything done to his hooves.

Supporting Characters

SIM: The family friend who drives Jason back to Vancouver from Red Deer.

SANKEY: Pedro's previous owner.

BUN BOLTON: The farmer who supposedly knows how to throw a diamond hitch, but instead directs the women to someone who actually knows.

MR. AND MRS. BURRELL: A young farming couple with a baby and a little boy. The women run into them randomly.

STANLEY BURRELL: The cowboy who actually knows how to throw a diamond hitch and is the brother of Mr. Burrell.

JOE: Works at Brewsters Stables and longs to join Phyllis and Anne on their adventure.

ART, MARTIN, AND THE DEACON: Part of the construction camp crew who remove Pedro's shoe.

MR. RICHTER: A mountain guide who was originally from Bavaria and helps the women navigate their way through the mountains.

MRS. McQUEEN: An elderly woman who welcomes the women into her home during the trip.

WALTER: An eccentric, grimy man with a warm heart who lets Phyllis and Anne camp out in his cabin.

CHARLIE: The purser on the ferry the women took from Victoria to Vancouver who bet them a case of scotch that they wouldn't make it back.

A Prologue

The diary left open,
            like a coil
                        of rope.

            Two girls in their twenties,
Phyllis and Anne,
                        took turns
                                    passing the book
                        and pen
                                    back and forth
                        between them

as they cleaved a way
                        through mountain passes

            from Victoria
            to Red Deer
            by roadster—
                        then back again
                        by horseback.

            Uncoil each strand of story,
then lash the lengths
                        and tie the knots
                                    to pull
                                                the tale
                                                            taut.

The book's pages fray
     and pictures
          slipped between
               shed loose.

    A newspaper clipping
        unbraids from the pages:
           a place
               to begin.

Monday, June 18, 1951

VANCOUVER, BRITISH COLUMBIA

PHYLLIS (LEFT) AND ANNE (RIGHT) IN JASON.

*"Got started and arrived at Vancouver all in one piece,
apparently only forgotten the maps."*
—ANNE

The Press

The reporter expects two girls:
curls fresh from rollers,
cherry-lipped photo smiles,
flowery blouses primly buttoned.

These girls roar in with crimson grins,
top of their car left down,
curls unstrung by the wind.

Phyllis in baggy flannel.
Anne, her white button-up
as crisp as the British accent
she calls out with.

The reporter imagined
a meticulous itinerary
planned for the trip.
The girls as cautious secretaries
tapping a timeline from typewriters.

When he asks,
Phyllis snorts:
Plan? There's no plan—
that's the point.

Their flippant answers,
their careless appearance,
push his plot off course,
the story veering—

A break
to take photos.
They slap on stetsons,
hamming it up atop
their 1927 MG Roadster,
a shared steed for the first phase.

In mid-pose he asks them
about their car.
Phyllis, straddling the hood
like a cowgirl,
leans forward,
palms pressed
onto the forest-green metal
and says:

> He has a
> full-floating
> rear axle,
> side valve,
> four cylinder
> engine.
>
> Magneto
> ignition
> three-speed
> transmission
> gravity-fed
> system.
>
> This is Jason,
> you got that down?

Jason's Christening

Phyllis and Anne
pool their cash for the car.
The latest owners
in a long line of ghosts,
they will hardly be the last.
Their time with the car
a brief chapter in his life.

Fragments of the past
matted in the metal,
stamped into the pedals.
A succession
of strangers' fingerprints
braided to the wheel.
Jason's legacy:
twenty years
of breath
by combustion.

With every stop
in village, town, and hamlet
park rangers and passers by ask them:
That thing from a museum?

But when he's hoisted
high on jacks, chrome
gleaming, a crowd grows,
the townsfolk lean in
like he's a freakshow spectacle.

With his top down,
he lets the wind buffet
the girls' sunburnt cheeks,
a relief from the heat.

On horseshoe curves
of secluded roads,
the girls pull over,
slide on shorts.
The rush of air
on their naked calves
is a cool caress,
a sweet freedom.
This forbidden act
indecent in front of
anyone but him.

Phyllis slices gaskets
out of rubber —
replacements to placate him.
Temperamental,
Jason demands
constant care.

While driving,
his erratic gauges
are a constant distraction.
Needles waver
to wild measurements
never to be trusted.
Anne says he growls
like a pregnant rabbit
up the passes.

His name a prophecy
given to them
upon inspection.
Father Bleathman,
at the Royal Oak garage,
wiping motor oil
on his overalls
told them:
You girls call him Jason now,
you call him Jason
'cause he'll fleece ya.

Instead,
they packed a toolbox,
learned to dissect
his iffy engine,
ready always
with the knowledge
for necessary adjustments,
their blackened hands
wiped on oily rags.

Hopalong on the Ferry

Phyllis

Hopalong Cassidy.
The policeman pointed him out,
boarding the ferry.

All I saw: a white stetson
bobbing
against the crowd.
Any closer and I'd have snatched it.
Forget his autograph—
I knew what I wanted.

The whole trip people gawped at us
until a couple came up
and asked for our autograph.
Newspaper stories
travel fast I guess.

They wanted our John Hancock
below Hopalong's:
You were sitting right by him at the shop,
didn't you notice? they prodded.

Only later
did Anne remember
the round-faced man
who grinned at us.
She thought him a dead ringer
for her bank manager.

All I could recall
was the woman next to him,
spoon sunk in a maple nut sundae.

Hopalong's too soft
to play a cowboy
anyhow.
You need a lean,
thin frame,
a hard line
of jaw,
a well-weathered
hide,
preferably scarred.
That's a cowboy.

Keremeos

The hotel and its broken
geography, up on jacks.
It squats, a battered shorebird,
knee-deep in black ooze,
a lagoon belching
fumes.

The stairs fractured
from the front door,
the girls jump the gap
on the hunt for a pay phone.

Inside, a congested hallway:
an office door
unhinged, drooping
against a wall;
a dresser with drawers
dangling from its sockets;
pockmarked curtains stained
by stale smoke.

Taunting, a pay-phone sign
points a path
to a large heap of bed linen,
cigarette burns pepper
the sheets like bullet holes.

A man's face peers
from a room down the way
Watcha looking for?
his words textured
by phlegm.

A pay phone.
Phyl rasps,
voice corrosive
with protective malice.
A harsh voice
masks fear,
lets a woman go
unchallenged
and untouched.

The man pulls
one swollen-knuckled
hand through hair
limp with sweat:
That'll be under the stairs.

They put the first call through
with the operator and sink
into a decaying couch
that sags
like a sullen smile.

Anne takes a drag
of her hand-rolled smoke,
Phyl toes the empty bottles
that corral the couch.

When Anne's call comes in,
she presses the receiver to her ear.
Her voice bright and lively
to ease her mother's anxiety.

Phyl waits and listens,
planning for her own call.
She'll share a handful of anecdotes,

leave out talk
of engine failures.

On their leaving,
another man
hangs haphazard
from the window:
You girls need a place for the night?
His pointed fingers
pick off and flick
flakes of paint
down at them.

Thanks, says Anne.
But, no thanks, says Phyl.
The window slaps
closed above them,
the corner of a curtain
caught and pinned
in the shutters.

Somewhere
from below the foundation,
a plumbing pipe vomits
excrement in response.

The Arrival

The mountain pass abandons
its swerves, cliffs and rock slides
and eases into foothills,
then prairie.

Anne, who moved to Victoria
via ship from London, England
had bypassed the Rockies entirely.
She watched in awe now
as the mountains planed
their hard edges
into the low roll of foothills,
to drop flush to flatland,
the sky a wide mouth
over the golden, bristled skin
of prairie fields.

Phyl had seen this process
from the reverse:
the ground building,
foothills, soft tongues
leading to glacial incisors.
All this on her last trip
taken from Tamarack Farms,
where her father, Herbert
had designed and
built the dairy barns.
Her mother, his business partner,
kept the books.
But a dairy drains you,
robs away your hours,
so Phyllis' parents

sold Tamarack
and retired to Victoria.

Phyl's return
prompted a string of visits,
from friends and family
she'd left behind.
Gossip traded over coffee
and their advice to her
on where to buy the horses.
All the while, Anne listened politely.
Slowed by her friend's old life,
she longed for open road.

Jason they dropped off
in a Red Deer body shop,
always eager to be pampered:
for repairs to torn seats
for a spiffy new side-lamp.
There he awaited
his guide for the drive back,
family friend Sim,
while the girls scoured
all of Alberta for horses,
following leads from friends.

They bought Monty, the pinto, for Anne;
Peaches, the roan, for Phyllis;
and a pack pony named Pedro.

Pedro's previous owner,
a withered man
named Sankey,
one tooth in his mouth
and his hat worn high
on his head.

He bewildered Anne by
saying: *Let's head to the house*
when they'd wheedled
out a deal.
Anne figured on the bigger
of the buildings,
with its high,
steeply pitched roof,
but Phyl tugged her
to the dilapidated hut
Anne had mistaken for
a chicken coop.
Anne stooped
under the low roof,
as Phyl put pen
to paperwork.

Anne said after,
that moment taught her
that in the West
a man
gives a bigger house
to his horses
than himself.

Throwing the Diamond Hitch

Grab the center of the rope,
    lay a length along the loin,
        the first line of the story.

Ball the lash cinch
      in your palm,
        throw it over,
            snatch it
      as it swings
          and hook it.

      Center the cinch,
       the story:
      two women
     on horseback
    and a pack pony.

Every hitch needs tension:
      two women
    in the wilds,

        alone.

Pull
    the rope
        taut.

As the line
    comes up
and over,
    start the twisting
        at the withers,
           weave
      other names
        within
      the narrative.

Now pull
    two loops:
      one onside,
      one offside,
    that catch
      the pack,
    twin snares
      for detail.

The ropes are crossing
      other tales, entwined
    at the top
      of the load,
    a diamond
      forming
    a web
of stories
    that surround
    the center:

    two women,
    three horses,
a cross country trip—

a simple thread
             that weaves.

Tie it with a packer's knot,
             loop over,
         swing under,
                      throw a half hitch.

             Anchor
             the tale
             to the panniers.

Friday, July 6, 1951

OLDS, ALBERTA

PEDRO (LEFT) AND ANNE ON MONTY (RIGHT)
AFTER CROSSING A CREEK.

Phyllis on the need to learn how to throw the diamond hitch:
*"Saddled up and got our pack tied on with a great deal of effort and
went off letting Pedro follow. Not very successful as he will eat and
then jog to catch up and the pack comes loose. It is not too secure, in
fact it is most insecure."*

Bun Bolton

In Water Valley, the rain hits.
Wet clothes cling to the girls
like leeches.
Their hair, slick tendrils of seaweed.
Their bodies create eddies
in the current of the rain.

The musk of horses
fuses with the cool air:
sweet clover sweat;
bruised grass breath.

Pedro, last of the bunch,
his pack hangs
lopsided to the left.
Anne glances back to check
that they haven't lost the lot of it.

The first stretch of their trip,
their pack listed and loosened.
They hadn't known they'd need a knot,
a special hitch that keeps a load
hugged to a horse's withers.
The diamond hitch: the packer's knot.

Their search for this knowledge
resulted in a string of names,
one supposed informant
leading them to the next,
and so far none of them
able to demonstrate the knot.

At the moment,
their present quarry:
a man named Bun.
Neighbors give varying accounts
of Bun's whereabouts.
The girls tramp
from farm to farm,
boots sinking
in a slurry of manure.

On finding his homestead,
the girls hunker down,
huddled under the eaves
of his shed, rain tapping
its fingers on the roof.

Bun arrives with a farmer's flair
aboard a chugging, rusty tractor,
its monstrous tires tearing
at the slurry of gravel.
A gnarled tree-root of a man,
his wizened, warm eyes
are full of wily glimmer.

Bun Bolton gives a tug
at the front door,
then welcomes them.
Grubby mugs line
the far counter.
Every picture
hangs askew
on the stained wall.

The girls stand,
dripping on the doormat,
as Bun crouches,
tinder in hand at the stove,
feeding the first flames
with newsprint and twigs.
The flush of heat spreads.
Bun flashes a grin to them across the room.
Make yerselves at home, he says
then ducks out to run some errands.

Phyl peels off
drenched socks,
and Anne follows suit.
They hang them
on the cupboard doors,
where they dangle,
elephant trunks
drooling rain drops.

Bun returns
rain in the creases
of his face.
He eyes the socks,
the jackets draped
on backs of chairs,
stetsons propped
up by the coffee pot.
He wipes a hanky
across his brow,
says:
Here's a disgusting sight,
then winks and leaves,
off to sleep
in a storage shed.

Over breakfast,
the cowgirls sip
coffee to the grounds,
while Bun admits
he's never known
the diamond hitch.

But there's a Texas cattleman,
goes by the name of Obern.
If they'd learn from anyone,
he'd be the one to teach
the throwing of the hitch.

Bun's directions
lack precision.
So with a shaky hand,
he draws a map.
The pencil jitters,
lines skittering off the paper.
His sense of scale
appears quite dubious.

His last act of kindness:
some added padding
to Pedro's cinch,
his best sock
cut up for the job.

Piebald Eyes Meet Their Match

The land refuses maps,
                         a rebellion against any
straight path on paper
                        that echoes the clear-cut,

            loggers driving
            steel
                        through the heartwood.

No trees here
                        would submit to being pulped,
to be laid flat
                        with measured markings
inked upon them.

The land takes
                        your plotted
            courses,
                        your reasoned
            routes
and ruins them.

            Bun's map:
                        a route
                                    scorched
            against the land's will.

            So it takes
itself
            and twists
itself,
                        distorts against description.

The hills that rise
                fold under and
      back.
The ground
      a lie,
      a film
            of solid soil
      stubbled
            by wild grasses,
but hooves
      cut through
the trick of crust.

      Peaches' hooves
              puncture the soil,
         sink into the mire
           of liar land,
    eyes wide
        and rolling,
    white half-crescent
           of fear
                framing the
         horse's irises.
    Limbs swallowed
    by the surface,
          strike up
             and out
    for a moment:
         slicing
            crazed
    arcs.

    Phyllis,
        shaken loose
           for a second,

lets the taut reins
                drop
                        slack,
        her body thrown back
and forth,
                lurching along
        with Peaches' twisting battle
                to free himself.

        Anne,
                her hand
        outstretched,
                helpless
                        through the struggle
                lets her palm
                        fall,
        as Peaches heaves
                        two feet
                                to solid land.
The mud belches its surrender.

                Equine brains
                                fritz
                        and falter
interpreting the terrain
        sopping and deranged.

Mud clings to their hooves,
                plaster-cast
        restraints,
                        the air encumbered
                                with the reek of muskeg.

In mincing
    steps,
      the horses test
        the ground,
the earth
    cradling
        hungry mouths.
    One hoof
        out of place:
    devoured.

The land slips
a trip-wire,
    a creek too deep
    to ford
      in most places.
The mud
    at its depths
      makes a twin battle
of suction and current.

    Women and horses
      follow its length,
Phyl's
    jaw,
      a taut line,
      an angle
    of bone
      beneath skin,
        the white jut
    of her knuckles.
Her eyes
    track
      the creek.

A gravel bar up to par
                for their fording,
                        Phyllis on track
                                down the bank,
        grateful
                for this stubborn jut
                        of land,
                hugging
                        the quick ribbon
                                of river.

                Pedro,
                        his hooves
                                sluice
                through the current,
                        an oozing slog
                                up the far bank,
                his muzzle buried
                        in a knoll,
                                grazing.

                Peaches
                        stutters.
                                His heels kick
                back
                        stones
                                that skitter
                        like teeth,
                                hooves grinding
                                        the rock
                                beneath.

Phyllis halves a bandana,   ties it to the bridle
                    and Peaches,
                              in his blindness,
                                        obeys.

                    Monty,
                              legs locked in refusal
                    his ear pin back
                              with every coaxing squeeze
                                        of Anne's heels.

          Phyllis passes the bandana
                              that Anne cinches tight.
          Phyl yanks the reins,
                              but no change —
                    Monty resolute.

          Phyllis retrieves
                              and swings
                    a half-rotten
                              fence rail
                              through the air,

                                        thinking a swift hit
                                                  on the hocks
          will jet the horse
                              into motion.
                    Monty gives a twitching kick
                    instead,
                              the board
                    snaps back
                              into Phyllis' shins

Phyllis yelps and grunts, spits out foul curses
                                        powerful enough
                to send bank scree
                                scuttering.

                She stamps to Monty's front end.

                Piebald eyes of the pinto
                meet their match
                in the woman's stubborn
                blue gaze.

Peaches towed back,
                an old pro at crossing.
The women bind a lariat,
        a tightrope
                between the two horses,
stretched
        thin and narrow
                        as their options.
Anne stands aside
                as Phyllis leads Peaches.

Monty, snugged
                to Peaches' haunches.
                        A click
        of Phyl's tongue,
                a yank on the reins
        draws Peaches forward.

Monty braces
all his weight,
                neck stretching,
                        muscle extended,

till the strain
                    breaks him,
one final tug,
                    a jump,
a landing mid-creek,
          the applause of splashing water.

Anne,   sidelined the entire time,
               sighs
               relief.

The Burrells

A quick glimpse
        of unexpected others:
    a young couple
        in a buck board,
    baby on the mother's lap
        and a grubby boy behind
   the father who drives
        the team of horses,
          slogging
            through the bog.

This family portrait,
        curtained
     and fractured
        by a frayed lace
          of tree limbs,
     as the family cleaves
          through the timber.

Phyl and Anne,
in a mad
    scramble,
hope to head them off
    and join them,
eager for direction
    across a hungry forest floor
        that sucks on horses' hooves.

The family, startled, still polite,
    invite the two for supper,
        for breakfast,
    a place to lay their bedrolls.

The Burrel cabin
runs backwards,
                built by Bun—
                        so no wonder.
            Metal siding
                    coated by cardboard
            surrounds two rooms:
                        a thin skin
            between this family
                        and the wind.

Mrs. Burrell strides
                between the table
        and the scalding range,
                            a canine efficiency.
        Her knife
                cleaves
                    thin slices
            of carrot,
                    making a supper for six
                    from a supper for four.

Mr. Burrell
            in from outdoors:
                    Your pack horse quarreled with our gate.
        His left hand,
                fingers blushed
                    with mud,
                        cups the mouth
                                of the pump
                                    near the door.
        His other hand
                    grips the handle,
        his arm
                with the awkward angle
                            of a heron leg.

He pushes,   pulls.
     Water
           spurts
                forth.

Phyl and Anne
       at the table
of halved logs,

unsure
of how to answer
mumble apologies
for the gate's destruction.

Anne grabs the dishcloth,
          a limp cadaver
               at the table's edge.

She balls it in her fist,
         begins scrubbing
           at a stain
                on the table's surface.

Two Kinds of Diamonds

Phyllis

Thickened spit clings to the bit and tries to drip, but stretches. The saliva necklace hanging from his horse's mouth, a prize for the trip back, forty miles from the seismograph outfit. Stanley Burrell pulls out a package, bacon bound up, fat licks the paper wrapping darker. He passes it to his sister-in-law, Mrs. Burrell. She grasps his gift: the greasy cliché brought home. His coming now, a knot of luck in the rope that we blindly follow to learn the diamond hitch. Before he'd come, I asked our question, Mr. Burrell, his brother, unable to name any other, said only Stanley would know how to cross the lines, the knots to tie, for the diamond hitch.

Anne dissuades me from asking Stanley to teach us now. She says nothing when she spots me, darting forward, my mouth half-open to inquire. Our eyes meet and a slight shake of her head and that's all that's needed to keep me silent. The man is exhausted after all and the light is failing us anyway. The dusk stains its way up the trunks of the trees as we walk back to the buildings. We share his bunkhouse. Anne and I pile on the mattress, Stanley lies on a bed of straw. He is the first to slip into dreams. First his breathing deepens, draws out in the length of its rhythms. Then the speaking starts, these soft mumbles Anne and I begin to listen for, interpreting his half-mouthed vowels. The two of us, too fascinated to sleep now, listening to all the odd things a man might say when dreaming.

At breakfast, we tease him about his sleep-talk. Won't tell him what he said. All his mumblings related to his job. He talked to his horse most, a low *Whoa* and a few *Gee-ups*. But we suggest instead scandalous tidbits until his face stains red.

Around lunch time, Anne finds Stan and me, polishing off a heel of rye whiskey behind a shed. She stands there, arms crossed, sulking at being left out despite my explanation. Clearly, we needed a smaller bottle for the rum, the slight flask of rye, a clear solution for a new container.

Stan catches Pedro, prepared now for the role of teacher, packs and ropes at the ready to show the diamond hitch. It takes effort for him to keep from working the ropes too fast. We lean against the fence rails, keen eyes tracking every movement. We shout and taunt him when he blocks our vision with his body.

He stands back, satisfied smirk, runs his fingers through the stiff fringe of his auburn hair, then thumbs the knots and pulls apart the pattern.

The two of us take on the task together, one on each side of the horse. On our first effort the ropes hang loose in parts, like picked threads in a sweater. The knots lop-sided and ugly. The second effort slightly better. He nods now, enough practice.

Girls, this diamond'll have to do. Until you get yourselves the real McCoy he says, voice played up to sound all coy.

Pedro

1.

Hank of timothy grass
hanging from his mouth,
stalks twitching
as his lips smack, punctuating
the rhythm of his chewing.

The crest of his neck sways
to the left,
a gesture of greeting
to every passing engine.

His casual amble
down the middle
of the highway.

2.

In Exshaw,
every door and window
left open,
a portal.

When he strays
they find him,
neck rounding
a door frame.

His shoulders
wedged
in the threshold
of a front door
left open.

The lips
of his muzzle
stretch and flap
at the handle,
like clumsy fingers
grasping.

Tourists

1.

A car perches on the shoulder,
a man swings open the side-door,
a string of kids and wife behind him.

His finger on the trigger
of his camera,
he clips pictures from the light.

The roadside attraction:
two weather-pummeled girls
in saddles,
the pack pony,
a mascot.

You girls leaving the country?

Phyllis and Anne
on their ambling mounts,
hooves dragging through gravel.

Phyl growls:
I know of quicker ways.

2.

From across the road
a man stands beside his car
and bellows:
Where you going gals?
his buttons straining
at the edges
of his shirt.
His lips wriggle
a cigar
side to side.

Anne, her calves bawling,
stomach knotted with hunger
calls back, terse:
Victoria.

Elephantine, his wife
in a green playsuit
smears a fuchsia tint
on puckered lips.
She stands behind him,
one hand balanced
on their car's front door:
Where you from gals?

After an hourly onslaught
of honking horns
on the highway,
passengers pointing
at the grimy cowgirls,
like paid attractions,
Phyl does not wish to reel in
the line of questions
sure to follow her answer.

She lowers the brim
of her white stetson,
tilts it till it cuts
right above her lashes,
snaps back:
Victoria.

The plump couple,
confused, then perturbed,
grumble, shuffle
back to the bench
of their car.

Saturday, July 14, 1951

BANFF, ALBERTA

ANNE COMMISERATING WITH MONTY.

"Arrived at the gates of the Banff Park in the pouring rain and were met by complete blankness when we asked about riding through. We had gone about a mile when a park warden in a green truck roared up and ordered us to come over and talk to him. Felt like small school children again. Our orders were to ride ten miles in to town, report at Brewsters Stables, and not leave town until we had checked in with the Chief Warden on Monday."

—ANNE

Welcome to Banff

A CONVERSATION WITH A PARK WARDEN

you cannot camp anywhere but in a campground
you cannot bring your horses to the campground
you cannot leave the horses
you cannot leave
until we say you can

Joe of Brewsters Stables

1.

Over the bucket, we strangle
sponges pulled from the water,
a snail trail of soap scum
smearing through grime.

Joe sits opposite,
colt legs crossed,
watching,
asks us our age,
where our mothers are,
and whether they worry.

Our sarcastic quips
in response,
a caustic armour.
We refuse to offer
any straight answer.

Joe,
his cowpoke face,
his stain of stubble,
his big, sad, soulful
eyes.

We rub towels
over arms,
around wrists,
erasing wet from skin.

We tamp our hats back on.
Accordion bellows
of sleeves slackening
down our arms.

Joe stands too,
his cowboy charm
to rise when ladies do,
his mouth half open
in question.
He inquires, half-hearted,
as if already expecting
a rejection.
He wonders
if he couldn't cajole us
into an evening trail ride.

We decline, as he expected,
explaining our exhaustion,
the thirty-two miles
we'd ridden that day.

His question,
a piston
churning pity
in our minds
through the night.

2.

Next morning finds us
bow-legged,
limbs rigid with ache,
back in the saddle,
dallying with him
to Sundance Canyon.

Joe,
aboard a mount
borrowed from the ranch,
calves clenching the horse's flanks,
hooves of his horse
an urgent metronome.
He strives to climb
to a sheep's cave.

We tie horses
near timberline,
devolve
to hands and knees,
clambering
along the incline.

He tires before his aim,
blames his stable job,
and its stresses:
dudes and their stupidity,
the boss and his demeaning
jabs, calls him simple-minded.

His ample grumbles
reduce to ambient hum,
our focus:
the land spread below us
spruce undulations
stippled with pine,
sectioned by scrawls
of gravel passes.

On the way down,
Joe sputters his solution:
he'd join us—

Youse kids 'ould not be sorry
if you let me come along,
and I'd not be a bit of bother.

We patiently remind him:
he has no horse,
he has no saddle,
he has no way
to have either.

Following the Wardens' Orders

Anne

Here we are at the wardens' office, just as they asked, and yet no one is here for us. The young English lad left to mind the place is perfectly useless. He shrugs and grunts minimal responses to our questions. The only thing he knows for sure: his supervisor is completely indisposed. A meeting we are told. He's in a very important meeting.

And so back we go into Banff. We shop for supplies, tins and packages, more to be strapped to Pedro's pack frame. We check the horses too. They pace, frustrated, in the barn, shake and bob their heads at us, paw the floor. I understand their feeling and find my anxiety strange. I am the girl from the big city after all. I have dealt with the unending hordes of London day after day, rushing from hospitals where I trained as a nurse. Banff and its tourist bustle shouldn't faze me and yet just one month with Phyl has changed me. As we tramp back to the wardens I find my eyes tracing the sharp line of the highway stretching off through the spruce. I fantasize about our escape.

Back at the office all the wardens have to offer is bad news. Our planned path, the shortest route, is walled off by four feet of snow. Completely impassable. We are forbidden from trying. Instead, we are to follow the main highway, departing at three a.m. If we leave any later we are an inconvenience to the motorists.

We take the wardens' plan back to Brewsters Stables. We relay when we'll leave as we pay the bill. *Absolutely not*, the stable boss says. *The barns are locked then and I'll not be opening them for you.* The boss will not relent despite Phyl's stubborn attempts at negotiation.

Joe finds us slumped against the barn with long faces, our paltry belongings clumped about us. *Three a.m.?* he says. *I can make that happen. I'll stay in the barn myself if it comes to it.* I am proud of Joe's rebellion against the boss he hates, but I won't allow him to take such a risk. If he were found letting us out at the crack of dawn he'd be sacked for sure. Joe agrees and instead will fix the barn doors for our escape. They'll look locked to any passerby, but when the time comes all we need to do is slip a hand through the gap in the door to lift the latch.

The second part of the plan: we spend the evening camped beside the horse's stalls, an action that is strictly forbidden. Dim lamps light our corner for only a brief moment when we bed down, and no prying eyes find us.

All night I lie awake, the saddle blanket lousy padding for a paved floor. The horses seem determined that I not drift off. Monty cannot decide between lying down or standing for sleep, alternating every fifteen minutes. And when at last he does settle, he begins to slap his lips, runs his long pink tongue over every inch of his muzzle. Does he dream of eating oats? And Pedro, fed up with one more night in his box stall, paws at the wall, rattling and thumping the boards. The twenty other horses boarded there snort and shuffle in the background. I close my eyes, remember the bliss of the cushy mattress back at my parents' house. I have dreamt of this bed often during our time on the road.

At some point Phyl nudges me, whispers, *It's time.* And I find I can't recall how long I've lain there, if I've slept or not. The whole night was a black haze fragmented by horse sounds and the ache of my body. My fingers are clumsy as we light the lamps and begin to pack.

When released from his stall, Pedro makes a break for a bag of oats in the feed room, but Phyl manages to snag him and ties him between Monty and Peaches. Sighing, he decides to satisfy himself by chewing Monty's tail as we pass the packing rope back and forth between us. Every time we pack our diamond hitch improves, ropes lay more evenly, knots less awkward. There are many who can tie this hitch on their own, but for us it is always a team effort. We have both memorized our role, standing on our side of Pedro, weaving the rope. I cannot imagine tying the knot alone.

As we creep from the barn the horses have never been more noisy. The clatter of hooves echoes off every outbuilding. We escape down a back road, sure at any second the stable boss will charge up behind us, threatening arrest. Instead, we move softly through the heart of the town. At this hour the streets are empty stretches of concrete. In the distance the mountains crouch like great, shadowed beasts. The air is so still I swear I hear them breathing.

Wednesday, July 18, 1951

MARBLE CANYON, BRITISH COLUMBIA

PEDRO (LEFT) AND PEACHES (RIGHT).

*"About two miles further on Pedro stopped and refused to go further.
We got him started again by whipping and pulling, but both felt
worried about the little guy. Finally reached our camp ground. After
we had eaten and washed up we started a game of Canasta and the
warden arrived with hay and half a sack of oats. Pedro still very lame.
Continued our game and were joined by ever increasing numbers
of men from the construction camp nearby. First, Art, a shifty,
shady looking creature. He could not sit still or look you in the eye,
and was very unshaven. He said the warden had been over
and told the camp about us."*
—ANNE

Removing the Shoe

Pedro, corralled,
               lame
     in his hind
        left leg,
                    he holds their party back,

              inflamed
                  hoof
                          suspended,
          tip
               pressing
                     half
               crescents
        in sand.

          Art and Martin
              and other
   construction camp workers
               gather,
     resting arms
              on fence rails.
   They offer suggestions.

Silent,
       the girls have decided
           to stick to the sidelines,
               pleased
                    with the workforce
           they've gathered.

A decision reached:
            remove Pedro's shoe.

Nine men vault the corral,
                    circling
                            around Pedro,
            Art and Martin
                        with ropes at the ready.

        At Pedro's head,
                    Art slips on
        the halter.

        Martin cuts
                        for the rear,
                rope in hands
                        for a sling.

        A pop
                    of pushed
                            air,
        a healthy hoof
                        cuts past
                                Martin's ear,

    and the camp deacon
                        runs to join
    Art at the front.

    The deacon's
            knuckles
                    hook
                            the throat latch.

Art's
　　　fingers
　　　　　braid to
　　　　　　　the cheek
　　　　　　　plate.

　　They hold Pedro
　　　　　　　steady,
　　　　　their legs spread
　ready
　　　　　as gunslingers.

　　Martin,
　　　　　side stepping
　　the posterior,

　　　　　the hiss
　　of Pedro's tail
　　　　　　　whipping,
　　　　　　　　　enraged.

Lunging
　　　for the leg —
　　　　　Martin
　　　　　　　clasps it
　　　　　　　　　at last.

　　Pedro rears,
　　　　　and careens,
　　　　　　　　off-balance
　　　　　his body
　　　　　　　crashing
　　　　　　　　　groundward.

Pedro,
            winded,
      cheek
            crushed
                  to sand,
      forelock
            smeared
                  over eye.

His nostrils quiver
            as he draws in
                  a deep breath.

      His flanks rise and fall
            at a slowing pace

                  and out snakes
                        his upper lip
                  twitching
                        for a blade
                              of grass.
      Anne and Phyl
            exhale in relief.

            Art
      and the deacon
            pull Pedro back
                  to standing.

Martin
        loops
the rope,
        hoof
                in hand now,

one palm
        on hock,
other pulling
                pastern,
            collapsing
the leg in
coiled
spring,
        the sling cinched
        tight.

All of Pedro's weight
            on the cannon bone
he's braced
            on Martin's knee;
Martin's right hand
            waves to the others
for nail pullers,
                passed nimble.

As Martin works the metal free
                the nails release
                        from the hoof's
                surface,
            steel fangs withdrawing.

The hoof naked now,
      free from the pressure
         of the metal.

          The shoe
             embosses
        the sand,

        and the men let go.

          And Pedro
             walks
               free.

Bacon Sandwiches

"WE HAVE DECIDED THAT FROM NOW ON WE WILL ALTER OUR MENU. WE WILL MAKE BACON SANDWICHES THE NIGHT BEFORE FOR BREAKFAST, AND THAT MEANS LESS DELAY GETTING ON THE ROAD IN THE A.M."

Phyllis

FRIDAY JULY 13

On waking, we find a low cloud has smothered our camp. The horses have vanished, but in the distance Pedro's bell clangs. We climb a ridge and see the silhouettes of other strays, not ours, half obscured by thicker tongues of fog. We find our ponies, clumped by the highway and pleased to see us, and we round them up and bring them back to camp, and we eat our bacon sandwiches.

SATURDAY JULY 14

We awake on a hillside near Exshaw. The mosquitoes have dealt fairly with us. They came, they bit, they left us in peace. The rocks we slept on were smaller than others we've suffered with and a rock slide didn't shoot us off down into the valley as we'd half-expected. We search for Pedro's bell, lost during the night, and find it sunken in the deep grasses of a ditch. We take the ponies down to the village for grazing, and as we watch them, we eat our bacon sandwiches.

TUESDAY JULY 17

This morning, we escaped from Banff. We left like criminals, stowaways in the stable, sneaking out with the horses at 3:10 a.m.

Long shadows etched across the stretch of empty highway as early dawn smeared across the sky. Only when we feel sure of not being caught, do we rest and eat our bacon sandwiches.

WEDNESDAY JULY 18

All night, Pedro's bell and its clanking cackle, as he inspects the surrounding camps and tents, muzzle snuffling against the canvas. We heard his teeth clipping grass, his lips smacking. We surrender at four a.m. pack and eat our bacon sandwiches.

THURSDAY JULY 19

The cook at the work camp across the way has taken pity on us. Rich tendrils of scents from across the road invite us before he does. Our knives sever the fluffy flesh of the hot cakes, as butter and syrup soak into the freshly made cuts. And eggs to the side, yolks a smooth yellow. And later for lunch an enormous ham is served, its bulk nearly breaking the table, and on the side plates home-baked bread, tomatoes bursting juice between our teeth. And for dessert fresh, plump cherries and sweet, sticky jam tarts and hot cinnamon rolls dripping with butter. We drown the lot with rich coffee.

SATURDAY JULY 21

Some of the fellows from the camp wake us, since we wanted to be up by 3:30. At 4:15, we found the horses; they'd pushed the bars from the corral and were out grazing. We gave them oats, and we ate our bacon sandwiches. Took a swig of rum too.

SUNDAY JULY 22

Slept till nearly five. Got up, and the ground was rigid with frost. We collected the ponies, our fingers seizing as they fastened buckles, slid to check the throat-latch and tightened girths. We ate our bacon sandwiches, drained what remained of the rum.

Barbed Wire

The women spot it
cresting the ridge
of the road ahead—
a claret hued
Eldorado.
Dust crescents
surge from its flanks.

The howl of gravel,
spat by tires,
that crow-hop
off the road.

Phyl and Anne
ride the horses
in the cradle
of the ditch,
their distance
from the road
measured
for safety.

While passing,
the car swerves at them,
the horn cackles,
flash of the driver's face,
in echo,
a man laughing.

The tight turn taken
too aggressively.
Tires bite the soft cheek
of gravel,
send the bonnet
plunging
toward them.

The horses jolt
to clear a path.
Anne and Phyl
are shaken in their saddles
but remain astride
and safely dodge the danger.

The car has cut
a black scar
through the grass
and come to a harsh stop
just short of the barbed wire
of a nearby fence.

The three boys
still in their seats,
ashen-faced
but unbruised.

Phyl glances back,
disappointed
with the lack
of carnage.

Braking and Blather

His plump thumbs
are paper weights,
pinning the map.
The heft
of his barrel body
thrown forward,
as his index finger
charts possible routes.

The map
is more for Anne and Phyl
than for him:
Mr. Richter, their savior.

The rangers sent the cowgirls his way.
Every mountain pass
Anne and Phyl were told of
at the last check in
with the rangers,
closed and impassable.
One ranger station
contradicting the other,
a breakdown
in communication.

And no wonder,
says Mr. Richter.
Those men know little
beyond their backyards.

For him,
every goat track
and clear-cut path
is a memory woven
within a synapse.

An ample Bavarian,
a mountain guide,
he traded Alps for Rockies,
his English words still coated
with guttural German.

He invites the girls
for an errand run
to Antler Lodge.
A load of furniture
had been dropped off
halfway there.
Dumped before a bridge
that wasn't yet completed.
Now, the construction done,
the load must reach
its destination.
A task the women happily assist with
as their ponies graze the pasture
in Richter's paddock.

The three of them packed
in his crew cab truck.
Bottles of beer
brought for the trip
jostle in the back.

They stop
at a colossal outcrop.

Mount Swanzy,
named for one
of Anne's kin,
she proudly declares.
The mountain's face
is painted tawny
by the last slants
of a fading sun.

The gravel artery
carves higher.
Dusk clutches
the valley below.
The truck rolls
to a halt.

A ranger lookout,
dwarfed by distance,
perches on a pine ridge
across the valley.
A fulvous glow haunts
its many windows.
The valley below
rolls out in dark waves,
a vast, dramatic expanse,
muted by the interwoven
boughs of spruce trees.
The three clink beers
to celebrate the view.

For the remainder
of their journey,
Mr. Richter steers
in intermittent stretches
to the washboards

at the roadside:
Invermere prattle,
tales of the townsfolk
too much distraction
in the telling.
He shares with them
the latest gossip:

There's the scandal
of that couple,
practically kids
when they'd married.
Two years in is when
it all came clear
to the young fella,
all those stomach aches
after hot lunches
packed by his wife,
no accident incurred
by poor cooking,
but her secret ingredient:
a teaspoon of ground glass
in every cup of stew.

Then the night,
a next-door neighbour,
flashlight in hand,
found Mr. So-and-So
stealing panties
from all the ladies'
clotheslines in town.
It's awhile ago now
since he packed up,
shamed into leaving town.

And that damned cabin
crouched on the outskirts,
the curtains always drawn,
never a soul seen outside
to mow that lawn; a jungle
looks awful shameful
next to the other houses.

With every tale told,
he pulls to the side,
slipping the key
to kill the ignition,
for meaty stories.

He can't balance
braking and blather,
gear shifts and gossip.

Near the summit,
headlights flash ahead.
A Japanese man
waves from his truck's cab,
pulls over, pops open
his side door.

The remaining beer,
four bottles,
reason enough
for rambling gab.
Their new friend Frankie,
a saw-mill man,
tells tales of the planer mill,
the nag of a boss
he calls Old Lovely.

At one a.m.
they stop to gather
the load left for the lodge.
The odd snort and snore
erupt around them
from the black juts
of canvas tents
huddled along the road.

The bridge to the lodge
freshly finished
by these invisible men,
present only
in grunts of slumber.

The load:
a few spindle chairs,
coffee tables,
and a chesterfield.

This new chattel
the girls heft
to the tailgate.
Richter's impressed
with the evenness
of their breath.

All three heave
the chesterfield,
but held
mid-air,
halfway from turf
to truck bed,
it converts,
mattress leaping

out, like a jack
in the box
bursting free.

Richter drops
his end,
leaps back,
as it lands
with a boom
against the truck's box.

Anne sucks breath
between her teeth
and listens
for the rustle
of grumpy, groggy men,
but the whistles of breath
wheeze on, unabated,
and Phyl and Anne
and Richter collapse
against the bumper,
convulsing in silent laughter.

Returning home,
and by his request,
Phyl's at the wheel,
her one slim wrist
resting on its rim,
the other hand
confidently steering.

Twelve Hooves Need New Shoes

Pedro first.
    He fights Phyl
    and the hired farrier
              like a fiend.

All that will calm him,
      ropes that cross and bind him

from his front shoulder
      to his hind leg

    and back again,
      a crude sling.

His pastern cradled
      in a Scotch hobble.

Phyl stands in front,
    holding the rope taut
      to keep the sling stable

    as the farrier
    gets down to work.

Pedro having none of it,
    flops to the ground.

    The struggle starts.
    As he thrashes,

Phyl's fingers

        work to

           hold the ropes.

Distracted,

      she doesn't feel

            the tail end of the line,

        the way the rope,

    has arced

      around

         her ankle.

Pedro's

   haunches

      burst

        against

        the rope,

  the trailing line

        pulls tight

          in a snap

             second,

       the scald

    of nylon

      as it saws

    through

      Phyl's muscle.

She writhes

      till the loop

          gnaws

            over

              her heel

      then, free.

Now, in the saddle
     her one foot
          dangles
               bootless,

          full
       of the fat warmth
          of swelling.

A Duet for Salmonella

1. Anne

We stop to pitch camp early, on the outskirts of Moyie, spread our blankets for a rest. Phyl chooses shade, while I bathe in sun. Sickness bleaches any flush from her cheeks. Her wan and waxy skin is cool and clammy against my palm.

With Phyl, hors de combat, I alone shift the pickets for the horses. I down a cold supper behind a copse of trees, guilty about eating with her darting to the bushes, retching and gasping in the long grass.

On my return from a scant meal, I find her curled on the bedroll, blonde curls lank with sweat, her eyes fixed blankly on a phantom object across the meadow. Non compos mentis, she mumbles for water, groans and turns away.

Canteen in hand, I mount Monty and head for the auto park across the road. The well dribbles up some rusty water first, but I pump it harder until it whooshes out clear. The canteen swallows it in great gulps.

On my return, Phyl takes small sips from the rim of the offered bottle. I overlap a pile of spruce boughs to soften her sleep. With her bed roll readjusted, she settles. She naps in snatches, her face flaccid, her sage lips sagging.

2. Phyllis

At four a.m. Anne's hand shakes my shoulder. After waking me, she thanks me for sharing my misery, my barely awake brain unable to untangle her meaning. She clambers off, cracking knuckles of knobby twigs, boots combing through knotted brome. I hear her scrunch to a stop, the gushing sound of upchuck glazing underbrush. My question answered.

A dank dawn smudges the sky. I've rolled Anne's limp body onto the spruce boughs, the sickly white of her cheeks gleaming against the dark fur of needles beneath them.

I lug buckets back and forth for our two faithful mounts to end their drought. The pack pony is nowhere to be found. The tubs slosh water on my thighs, white motes drift across my vision. And while I re-hammer tethers, I spot Pedro. He's reclined along the dividing line of the highway. His nose planted on the blacktop rumbling wet snores.

Torrent

Anne

The mountains gut
the storm cloud.
The torrent batters tree limbs.

And we stack staves of cedar,
tuck the tarp over them,
huddle under.

My wet fingers grip
a cold can of beans.

Morning:
sodden bread a pulp
that clings to my teeth and gums.
Feet burp into sodden boots;
saddle pads slap
the wet backs of the horses.

As I ride,
wet denim rubs
a rash into my thighs.

I long for a hot tin cup
of coffee to cradle
in my stinging palms.

From the Eaves

Phyllis

> While we pass regimented
rows of houses,
> > raindrops pummel our stetsons.

> Beneath the eaves,
women cluster,
> > their skirts unsullied by the mud.

> This mute group
of Doukhobors
> > observe us.

> Our shoulders stiff
with shivering,
> > we meet the group's gaze.

> They clasp their hands,
draw back indoors,
> > kerchiefs
> > > obscuring
> > their faces.

Thursday, August 9, 1951

KASLO, BRITISH COLUMBIA

PHOTO TAKEN JUST OUTSIDE OF KASLO.
PEDRO (LEFT), PHYLLIS ON PEACHES (CENTER),
AND ANNE ON MONTY (RIGHT).

*"Pedro is very excited with Kaslo and whinnied everywhere he
went on main street. Went off to buy groceries and left Pedro tied
to the telegraph post, came back to find the blacksmith riding Pedro
up and down main street. Pedro was being very much the arab,
head up and hoppety, jogging up and down the road."*
—ANNE

Mrs. McQueen

Phyl knocks at a cottage. A voice from indoors, bright but fragile, calls for her to come on in. Phyl says she'd be happy to if she weren't tethered to a horse.

A woman peeks from halfway up the door, her forehead crowned by silver curls. On the porch before her stands Phyl, reins over one shoulder, and behind, a roan plucking at her stetson. A section of steel frame, the body of a wheelchair revealed when the woman opens the door wider.

Mrs. McQueen offers pasture for the horses, a corner for the luggage and welcomes them in. Deftly, she navigates the narrow corridors, her forearms lean with muscle. Her fingers rise to her mouth, as if to press in a laugh, or put a stopper in the empty bottle of a question.

She has more daughters than rooms, each with a husband and children in tow. Her girls slip on six brightly patterned aprons and lead Anne to the orchard. Their faces echo their mother's with slight variations: cheeks rounder, noses sloped at different angles, eyes farther apart. They ring around the ladder that Anne climbs for cherries, direct her as her fingers pinch fruit from the twigs. They laugh as they rush to catch the ones that she drops in pouches formed when they lift the edges of their aprons.

When Phyl and Anne gather their things to leave, they will find a bag nestled next to theirs, cherries bubbling out the top. One falls, rolls a distance, dragging its nectar behind it.

Getting Directions

Bunched cars
    at the junction.

Horns squawk
    with ire.

Pedro stands in the center,
    his eyes fixed
on the road sign
        he reads
            for directions.

Sandon Mine

The rain abates, the air left dank and sweet with spruce breath. Madid moss in the ditch holds the imprint of hooves.

Anne's finger becomes a baton, tipping its point to each wildflower that she spots. She chants their names, an incantation of gratitude for the end of the rain.

Phyl is deaf to this roll call of flora. She gives a surly jerk, as she strips sodden gloves from pruned up joints, puffs warm air into palms. A halo of steam encircles her face.

A cyan Ford sedan crawls by. Its tires on gravel, like molars grinding cubed ice. The passenger window rolls down, a slit, so a man can call: *Like a drink?*

The driver pulls over, and Anne and Phyl dismount. The men say they are workers from the Sandon mine. They pass a beaten glass bottle of rum and coke to the women, which the two gladly share. The men say they slowed, for they knew them somehow. Hadn't they seen them at the hotel up the road?

The rum runs its hot fingernails down the girls' throats, sours in their empty stomachs. Anne's eyes gone glassy, she laughs too much at the men's feeble jokes.

The men say, *Leave your horses at the camp. Come with us to Nakusp. We'll buy you t-bone steaks. We'll take you to the sauna.*

Anne can almost taste the seared steak; Phyl can almost feel the flush of warm water. Then Anne's rain-slick fingers slip on the bottle. A frantic grasp and she clutches at the neck before the glass is dashed. Phyl shakes herself back alert, tells the men no and sends them on to their camp to inquire after a farrier. Phyl tosses the bottle off into the underbrush.

Blue Ford Déja Vu

A next day déja vu
with the blue sedan,
alabaster faces
of the miners
calling out
an identical offer:
to abandon their horses
for saunas and steaks.

Bellies packed
with camp breakfast,
the girls shake their heads.

And Pedro,
      weary

           with the car's cajoling crawl,

    pulls past
        rump swaying
            in the center.

When the Ford,
    close behind,
        seeks to pass him

           his hindquarters
   grind
     against the bumper,

edge the sedan
               deftly

                              into the ditch.

Pedro rejoins the others,
the press of the fender,
a dimple, the only residue
nearly vanished.

The Boot Maker

The boot maker
strums the tanned hide,
knife in hand.

Shoe-forms
and leather scraps
litter the shop floor,
soles beaten to the quick,
ready to be stripped back
and reattached.

His old friends sit with him,
their backs sloped in lazy crescents,
their conversation traded
over coffee gripped
in raspy hands.

The boot maker's shoulders,
permanently stoop
over his pot belly.

In his stained palms,
the lace leathers,
the ties for the latigo
that the girls were searching for.

Tuesday, August 14, 1951

BURTON, BRITISH COLUMBIA

PHYLLIS AND WALTER STANDING IN FRONT OF HIS CABIN,
HIS MODEL A PARKED BESIDE THEM.

"Walter was tall and limp and grimy, much the same colour from his boots to his hair. He had occasional teeth and an enormous pair of overalls that, although he was really quite a big man, made him appear very lean. Walter used to brew moonshine at Pine Lake and knew old Sankey who raised Pedro. Of course that made us old friends and we soon found that plans were being made for us and the ponies."
—PHYLLIS

Planting

Walter's cabin slumps, resigned to the earth edging up its sides, engulfing it into a stomach of soil. In a matter of decades maybe only the razor's edge of the roof will be left crowning from the earth, like a long splinter emerging from skin.

Inside, a tub huddles in the middle of the main room. Walter refers to it fondly as his rubbish dump. Empty tins and assorted garbage, eggshells and coffee grounds, spew over its edges. Anne notes the way that the calendar pages have tiled the floor. The assorted dates beneath her feet tell her the place hasn't seen a dustpan or mop for a full two years.

Walter stoops his tall frame on a stool, passes Anne and Phyl hot brandies. He grins, showing his occasional teeth, then starts in on his stories:

There was Ole Dusty. He and two other fellas were up in the hills hunting when the storm blew in and they couldn't light a fire for the life of them. Either the wind huffed it out, or the rain spat on it. No chance in hell of keeping warm that way. Three darn fools with rifles. They each picked themselves a tree, walking 'round it all night to keep warm. Well Ole Dusty, he got tired and set hisself down. Next morning they found him froze to death. His friends hiked out and got a pack horse and come back after him. They lashed him on one side and shot a goat to tie to the other. They wanted some meat anyway. And when they got down with Ole Dusty we planted him.

Then there's the old boy who built this cabin. He had an awful nagging wife so's he took to spending most of his time up in the hills. I likes to too you know. I sets up there, high as I can get just to get a good view of the situation all around. Makes me wish I could draw or paint or something to catch all that beauty. But I just goes up there to think most times and that's what he did too. Finally one September he came out. Guess he found hisself a solution to his problems up there. His wife took to nagging him again an' before Christmas we planted him. Found him in the woodshed. He'd braided a good sturdy rope for hanging. He was always so darned good at braiding and doing knots and things of that kind. Still, none of us could figure why he wouldn't have just used his gun and done the job that way. But I 'spose he was kinda known for being a terrible shot and that'd be the worst time to fire a bullet in the wrong place.

An' I gotta tell you about the three boys who went up into the hills prospecting awhile back. Well when they'd gone a considerable distance up the trail, wouldn't you know it but one of their damned dogs had followed them up there. That dog would not go home and they allowed it, by force of circumstances, to follow them up to their camp. When they'd got themselves all good and settled in camp the three of them drew straws as to who was to dispose of the dog. The man for the job was picked and off he goes with the dog into the woods. He thought dynamite'd do the trick, tied three or four sticks of it around the poor hound's neck with the caps on the other side, then lit the fuse and kicked the poor thing off into the trees. He was damned happy to see it hightailing it away from him. But then he gets hisself back into camp and hears all kinds a strange noises. Damn dog went running right back for the cabin and hid hisself under the bed. So the other two fellas were yelling and screaming and running up the trail away from the place. Next morning they came and had a look at all the damage in their camp. Not a proper bit left of that dog otherwise we'd 'ave planted him too.

Anne and Phyl, their cracked mugs of brandy emptied, are relieved to find the stories of planting at an end. A bag of apples placed near their pillows drives away the fetid stench of the house. Anne swears she feels the house sinking and says so. Phyl nods in agreement, face drooping with fatigue. They drift off to sleep, the foundation nosing deep into the underground.

Okanagan

The sprinklers echo crickets
with twitching rhythm.
Faucets spatter the orchards,
while in the distance
sage brush dabs
the arid foothills
left untended.

Anne cups a peach
in one palm,
her teeth plunged
to the pit,
lips pursed
and sucking.

The juice that drips
from the peach
is honey hued.
Anne's fingers, wrists,
wet with it.
The sultry air
stirs the scent from her skin,
transforms it to perfume.

Banners

Houses adorn the brow of a hill.
Churlish and weary,
Phyl and Anne
rest just below,
where the incline
eases to horizontal.

A woman approaches
from the homes above.
She huffs out breath,
her cheeks puffed out.
In her arms, a baby
sucking his way
through a swaddling blanket.

Hello down there! she calls.
Don't think I've seen you two before.
She crouches,
perches the baby on her knee.

Everyone's been telling me
they haven't seen a baby more adorable.
Just look at these cheeks!
Her thumb dimples his face
as though it were warm dough.

Phyl and Anne nod,
smile politely.

He has his father's face you know.
Everyone says that too.
But you don't see Daddy much do you?

She wiggles him on her knee.
His father's a demolition expert,
she says.
She hasn't even mentioned her name,
or asked for theirs.

Daddy's job is full of dangers,
yes it is, she coos to the baby.
The phone company
hired him awhile back.
He helps blast
through the rock
so's they can put the line through.

Anne pushes a yawn off
with the heel of her palm.
Phyllis scalps the grass
with a free hand
to keep alert.

And you two are travelers, she continues.
I can tell.
I used to travel too you know.
I'm terribly well-travelled.
Not like the folks here you know.
The folks here are too afraid
to even go to the next town over.
I'm afraid I'm nothing like them,
I just can't relate
because I came from Vancouver.
I'm too cultured for them you see.

The baby turns fussy:
crumples his hands to fists,
his mouth erupts
in a squall.
His mother rushes
him away.

Grateful for the relief of silence,
the women drift into a mid-day slumber.

The thump
of hooves on grass
wakes the women.
Anne catches a last flash

of Pedro,
        trundling away over
                a neighboring hill:

the woman's clothesline
                        drapes
                his shoulders.

Flannel diapers
                        flutter
        like banners

                before he vanishes.

The Home Stretch

Hooves drum
the pavement
in the midst
of a mass
of traffic.

Power lines cleave
the late evening sky,
landscape blocked
by tall offices,
the unending line
of buildings,
a border
for the trip
down main street
Vancouver.

The horses endure
trolley buses
and traffic lights,
but skitter
when sparks fly
off wires overhead,
as a trolley passes.

Visible at the city limits,
a grey streak of ocean
stretching off into mist,
the ferry at the dock
waiting.

Filling the Last Gaps

The diary ends on the ferry-ride home. The last stretch of the trip to Victoria, their homecoming, perhaps considered too bland by Anne and Phyl to capture. The reason might have been fatigue, the many months they'd rode, writing portraits, capturing the quirks of each character braided into their tale. Or maybe melancholy stopped the flow of ink. The ferry's slow glide to their island home, the journey's end a certainty that they didn't want to pen.

The diary ends with a man named Charlie, bouncing into the ferry cabin. Exhausted, they'd snuck out of the cocktail party thrown in their honour on the ship's deck. Their time on the road had made them introverts and the rowdy crowd was too much for them, so they retired for the night to sleep. Charlie, left out of the tale somehow until now, was a purser they'd met. On the first half of the trip, they'd told him of their scheme while boarding the ferry. He'd made a foolish bet their plan would founder and fall to nothing. But if not, he'd buy the cowgirls a full case of Scotch. He looked shocked to see them saddle sore, but triumphant on the ferry back, but promised to settle his debt. It was a while before he did, but Phyllis remained indignant about it long after. Twelve bottles of scotch make up a case. They were given twelve alright, twelve one-shots, all stood up on blocks of wood in a hollow meant for a large bottle.

				B.C.C.S. 461-12		FREIGHT BILL and/or ARRIVAL NOTICE **1**

FREIGHT BILL and/or ARRIVAL NOTICE **1**
B. C. COAST SERVICE
To the CANADIAN PACIFIC RAILWAY COMPANY Dr.
For Transporting the undermentioned freight
FROM VANCOUVER WHARF, B.C. (9771) TO VICTORIA WHARF, B.C. (9979)

S.S. PRINCESS
JOAN   DATE **SEPT 26/51**   IN PRO.   W/B NO. **76450**
SHIPPER and CARTAGE CO.
MISS A WILSON   C/B 599
CONSIGNEE and ADDRESS
MISS A WILSON   VICTORIA BC

No. of Pkgs.	ARTICLES AND MARKS	WEIGHT	RATE	FREIGHT	ADVANCES	PREPAID	COLLECT
3	**RIDING HORSES**		**3 @**				
			9 00 EACH	**27 00**			
			CR	**12**		**27 12 PAID**	
	DOLLIE No.						

WRF   Received Payment, ____ 19__   **27 12 PAID**   Agent.

Make Cheques Payable to Order of CANADIAN PACIFIC RAILWAY CO.
Mail to Wharf Freight Agent

Jason was driven home by their friend Sim, and all through the fall the women rose early to ride their horses through the frost of dawn. But when the snow came, Phyl sold Peaches, and returned to Red Deer to marry Bud, the boyfriend she left behind. Bud was clever. When Phyl and her family left the farm he'd bought her best mount, Red. *She'll be back one day now that I've got her horse,* he told their friends. After a while Anne was married too, to a man named Neil, and left for Prince George. Pedro was sold to a girl to help her with a paper route. The women imagined that, after a little time, he had the route down, delivered the papers on his own.

Epilogue

Every hitch thrown
      makes a fleeting story
            from a line of rope.

    Pry loose
        the knot,

           and the line
                falls slack,

    but coil it,
        and you find the fray
                of abrasion
      the kink
          where two lines
      crossed.

      Every rope remembers
      the tale of its tying.

A Note

Phyllis was my granny, and Anne was her best friend. The poems in this book are based on the travel diary they wrote during their 1951 ride. A few liberties have been taken here and there with some minor details, but the quotes accompanying the photographs are taken verbatim from the diary.

Phyllis and Anne remained lifelong friends. Whenever I saw them together it was like they were back in their twenties again, teasing each other and making quirky jokes. At my granny's funeral, Anne spoke of their 1951 ride and what it had meant to both of them. At the time they told people they had wanted to buy horses, and wanted to take a horseback ride that lasted longer than a day. But Anne talked about how it was a last hurrah for both of them as single women before they settled down and got married. Anne said she hadn't really known what she was in for when they left on the trip, but it gave her a deep sense of strength and independence that she drew from during her life.

Acknowledgements

Earlier versions of some of these poems have appeared in the magazines *NōD, untethered, Matrix, Touch the Donkey, One Throne, Freefall, Blue Skies,* and *Wax: Poetry and Art Magazine*; the chapbooks *Pedro* (Papertiger Press), *Braking and Blather* (above/ground press), and *Throwing the Diamond Hitch* (no press); and the anthologies *The Calgary Project: A City Map in Verse and Visual,* and *The Calgary Renaissance*.

I would like to thank my first poetry professor, Joan Crate, who read a very early start to this book and helped set it on its path. A big thank you to everyone in Christian Bök's manuscript-length poetry class—their helpful critiques were essential to making this book what it is. I'm very grateful for Christian Bök's guidance, and for the extra time he took after class to provide me with additional notes and feedback in preparation for submitting my manuscript for publication. To Richard Harrison, Aritha van Herk, rob mclennan, and derek beaulieu: thank you for your advice and kind support of my work. Thank you to Helen Hajnoczky, Melina Cusano, and the rest of the crew at University of Calgary Press for helping make this book a reality.

One of the reasons Calgary is very dear to my heart is the fantastic writing community that we have here. Thank you to the NSWGFTIAVI—many late nights were spent at the KP with you working on these poems. To my writer friends, far and wide- you feel like family to me and I'm so grateful for all of you.

To my parents, Linda and Grant, and my brother, Tim, thank you for always being so supportive and genuinely excited about my work.

And of course, thank you to my granny, Phyllis. I really wish that you were around to see this book come out. It's not the feature film that you and Anne had hoped for, but I think you'd both get a kick out of it nonetheless.

About the Author

Emily Ursuliak writes both poetry and fiction. She holds an MA in English from the University of Calgary, and a passion for literacy and her chosen career, librarianship. She is the host and producer of CJSW's literary radio show, *Writer's Block*, where she interviews authors, records readings, and peers into the private libraries of Calgary book lovers. She calls Calgary, Alberta, home. *Throwing the Diamond Hitch* is her first book.

Granny Phyllis (left) and Emily (right)

Brave & Brilliant Series

SERIES EDITOR:
Aritha Van Herk, Professor, English, University of Calgary
ISSN 2371-7238 (Print) ISSN 2371-7246 (Online)

Brave & Brilliant publishes fiction, poetry, and everything in between and beyond. Bold and lively, each with its own strong and unique voice, Brave & Brilliant books entertain and engage readers with fresh and energetic approaches to storytelling and verse, in print or through innovative digital publication.